SUSPENDED ADOLESCENCE

Understanding and Dealing with Teenage Substance Abusers

Richard P. DeSantis, PhD

Gerald J. Manney, MS, CADAC II, LADC I

Revised 2007

Pages 10-25 are adapted from
"Someone I Know Drinks Too Much,
and It Scares Me."
G. Manney, M. Kunhardt
Beech Hill Publishing, Dublin, NH 1983.

Illustrations in Chapter 7 by Richard P. DeSantis PhD.

Cover design by Erik Stackhouse

ABOUT THE AUTHORS

Richard P. DeSantis, PhD, is full professor emeritus of Health Sciences and former chair of the Health Sciences Department at the University System of New Hampshire – Keene State campus. Dick served as a member of the faculty from 1970 to the spring of 2004 and has worked and presented in the field of addictions and co-occurring diagnosis for more than 35 years. In addition to teaching upper division preparation courses at both the graduate and undergraduate levels, his experience includes serving as a consultant, lecturer, and staff person at various treatment facilities and specialized hospitals, primarily for the treatment of addictions. Dr. DeSantis held his license as an alcohol and drug counselor until 2005 when he retired from service, but continues to do trainings for professionals in Florida and Maine.

Gerald J. Manney, MS, CADAC II, LADC I, has worked in the substance abuse field for more than 35 years. Jerry is a nationally certified alcohol and drug counselor and a Massachusetts licensed alcohol and drug counselor. He is clinical supervisor for a Substance Abuse Mental Health Services Administration (SAMHSA) Effective Adolescent Treatment grant (MET/CBT 5) at The L.U.K. Crisis Center in Fitchburg, Massachusetts. He had been an adjunct instructor in the undergraduate division at Keene State College and an adjunct instructor in the Continuing and Graduate Education Department of Fitchburg State College, teaching courses *The Impact of Alcohol and Other Drug Dependencies upon the Family System* as well as on substance abuse disorders. He has been published numerous times in professional journals; his primary focus is on understanding and supporting parents of substance-dependant adolescents. He is also author/publisher of the website suspendedadolescence.com.

This book is especially dedicated to the

memory of Eric and his family.

ACKNOWLEDGEMENTS

We appreciate the time and information shared with us by Paul Madden, MEd, Alan M. Jacobson, MD, and others from the Joslin Diabetes Center, Boston, Massachusetts. We are thankful for Margee Kunhardt's permission to adapt *Someone I Know Drinks Too Much and It Scares Me* for use in chapter one.

The PAIN/FUN circles in Chapter 1 were adapted from a presentation by the late Father Robert Donohue, PhD.

We are also grateful to John D. McPeake, PhD, whose encouragement and support was instrumental in the first edition of this book.

We are especially grateful for the many parents who offered feedback, comments, and suggestions along the way. A special thanks go to Jill Nye, Polly Bannister, and Marilee Nihan for their contributions. Without the help of all of these people and more, ***Suspended Adolescence*** would have remained in a state of suspension.

Steven LeBlanc, Erik "Pir" Stackhouse and Sarah Johnson were vital in bringing the revised edition to life.

TABLE OF CONTENTS

INTRODUCTION

Today's youth "now love luxury. They have bad manners and contempt for authority. They show disrespect for their elders and love chatter in place of exercise" [Socrates circa 400 BC]. From the time of the ancient Greeks, and most likely before, adolescence has been a period of turmoil. It is also a time of growth for the teenager ***and*** the parent as well. ***Alcohol and other drug abuse changes that.*** Alcohol and other drugs can exacerbate the "normal" mood swings, depressions, rebelliousness, and acting out behaviors of adolescents, and prolong them indefinitely. Drugs taken repeatedly may delay or slow down emotional growth, ***LEAVING THEM IN A STATE OF SUSPENDED ADOLESCENCE.*** The most hopeful aspect about adolescent-onset substance abuse or dependence is that they are treatable. However, the added tragedy is that alcohol and other drug or substance dependence are probable the most misdiagnosed illnesses. Mary (not her real name), the mother of a recovering alcohol and drug-dependent son, states:

> "Our nightmare lasted for four years, and my son's addiction was like a cancer that infested the whole family. It slowly ate away at us all and would have completely destroyed our family had we not gotten help."

While removing asbestos from buildings may prevent certain cancers, it does not help once cancer has already developed. Once cancer occurs, it has a life of its own. It then takes accurate diagnosis, treatment, and ongoing support to effectively deal with it. It's similar to effectively dealing with substance dependence. Even if the cause or contributing factors of an individual's substance abuse could be documented, ***once it progresses to dependence, it takes on a life of it's own.***

> "In our family I was the great enabler—boy, how proficient I became at it. I allowed my son to do things I would never allow his brother or sister to do, and I allowed it out of fear, afraid that if I didn't give in, he would run, and I couldn't stand the thought of that. He knew full well how I felt and knew my fears and took every advantage of that. I also lived with denial for many years. I knew my son was using, but I kept trying to convince myself that it would pass, that it wasn't as bad as it seemed, and that our lives weren't out of control. And the one night out of ten that he came home on time and sober, was enough to reinforce that thought."

Alcohol and or other drug dependence can leave families in a state of turmoil. Misinformation and fear are the greatest allies of substance dependence. Knowledge, appropriate treatment, and support are its greatest enemies. As Mary put it so well: "Today, as a result of the help and support my family has received, I am able to refer to the bad times as, ***that was us*** instead of ***that is us.***"

We hope that the families who read this book will be able to share that same sentiment. We write this book as a way of helping you and your teen grow in health and love.

PART I

IDENTIFYING THE PROBLEM

Chapter 1

THEY ARE SICK KIDS, NOT BAD KIDS

Ed and Lynn are parents of a 16-year-old girl, named Kim. They have been increasingly concerned about her behavior: breaking curfews, a significant drop in grades, and frequent arguing. They suspect she has been smoking marijuana, and they smelled alcohol on her breath a few times. When they first started seeing their family counselor, Jim, they were angry, scared, frustrated, and just worn-out. Jim reviews with Kim and her parents the Federal Confidentiality Regulations (U.S.), which protect information that a client, age 12 or older, shares with a counselor as part of substance abuse counseling.[1] With few exceptions, such as if it appears that Kim was actively suicidal, has been abused by an adult, is threatening to harm a particular individual, and some other exceptions, Jim will need Kim's written consent to release any information about their individual counseling sessions, even if Kim's parent are present at some sessions. Jim understands that these regulations are critical in developing trust with substance- abuse clients. Jim meets with Kim individually for a few sessions and assesses that Kim's main problem meets criteria for marijuana dependence. Kim agrees to have Jim meet separately with her parents. She authorizes, in writing, that Jim can disclose to her parents her diagnosis and his recommendations, but tells Jim "don't tell them how much I was using or if I have used recently." (Some therapists and clients prefer to have the adolescent see a different therapist than the one the parents meet with.) Jim schedules another session to explain this to the parents. In the meeting, Ed and Lynn react with anger at first.

Ed: You mean my daughter is a drug addict? Hey, listen, that's my child you're talking about! She's no addict! What Kim is, is disrespectful. Her grades are slipping, and we don't like the kids she's been hanging around with. She needs a good swift kick in the rear.

Jim: Alcohol and other drug dependencies are illnesses. Kim is a sick kid who needs help … not a bad kid who needs to get punished.

Fortunately, Jim has a good understanding of how parents can be affected by serious illness of a son or daughter. [*See chapter 2, "Understanding and Coping with Chronic Disease.*"] He sees Ed and Lynn's anger as normal reactions from tired, frustrated, and very concerned parents. The anger, however, now threatens to entrap and engulf them in a draining downward spiral of confusion, anger, despair, and blaming.

Lynn: I've tried everything—pleading, threatening, yelling, ignoring—but ***she keeps drinking alcohol and smoking marijuana!*** I can't stand it anymore! She knows how much this bothers me. If she loved us, she wouldn't keep drinking and using drugs.

Jim: Love has little, if anything, to do with it. Although she may have begun to drink and use drugs out of curiosity, peer pressure, or to cover up her feelings, she now continues to drink and use because she has an illness: substance dependence.

Ed: An illness? Baloney! She just acts that way because she doesn't care. How can using drugs be an illness? She didn't catch it from someone.

Jim: I know this can seem confusing. Let me try to explain. Would you accept measles, mumps, and chicken pox as illnesses?

Ed: Sure. I've had all of them as a child.

Jim: What about heart disease or cancer?

Ed: Yes, of course. Everyone knows that.

Jim: If I had heart disease or cancer and I sneezed, would you get my illness?

Ed: [*Laughs*]. No, of course not.

Jim: An illness is basically anything that causes a change in the normal functioning of any part of our body. Certainly alcohol or other forms of drug dependence not only disrupt the normal functioning of the user, but also affect the people around them. We don't know the cause of every illness, and we don't know what causes alcoholism and other drug dependencies. ***[See chapter 5, "Why My Kid?"]*** We *do* ***know that substance-abuse disorders and substance dependencies affect about 9.1 percent of people age 12 or older (in the U.S) directly and at least three to four times as many people like you indirectly.*** [2]

Ed: If Kim has an illness, why doesn't she admit it and quit using? I think that's a cop-out.

Jim: First of all, almost all substance-dependent people need help to stop drinking and or using in order to stay clean and sober. Secondly, and most importantly, ***they usually don't understand that their drinking or drugging is the problem.***

Ed: You have got to be kidding. Our whole neighborhood knows! I am beginning to think we made a mistake by coming here.

Jim: Could you just stay a little longer? I think it will begin to make more sense very soon. *[Ed nods his head and isn't sure he wants to stay, even though he doesn't know where else to turn. He looks at Lynn and feels a little self-conscious about getting up and walking out].*

Jim: Most people react in similar ways to very bad news. Our mind tries to protect us from significant emotional or psychological pain by automatically using ***defense mechanisms.*** We may tell ourselves, "it isn't true," or "this can't be happening to me," or "I can't believe it." We call this denial.

Lynn: You mean lying?

Jim: No, it's quite different. Lying is attempting to keep the truth from someone else. Denial, when used as a defense mechanism, is used to keep the truth from ourselves." You may say to yourself*:* ***I don't want to believe that something bad is happening to me.*** If I admit that I might have a serious problem or illness, whether it's cancer, drug dependence, or something else, then I am also acknowledging that I might not get better. That's frightening, and at first I don't want to face that.

Lynn: I can relate to that. When I heard that my friend died unexpectedly, I remember thinking: "no it can't be" and "there must be some mistake."

Jim: Exactly! As family members, we also use denial, saying things like ***"I don't want to believe that something bad is happening to someone I care about!"*** I tell myself: "She's not addicted," "She'll outgrow it," and "It's just a bad habit."

Lynn: I've done that, but the problem didn't go away. Sometimes she would seem better and then later her behavior would be worse than ever.

Jim: That's the progression of alcohol or other drug dependencies. Without help, it gets worse. ***With help, however, alcohol and other drug dependencies become very treatable.***

Lynn: You mentioned denial. It seems so much greater with her than with other illnesses.

Jim: That's usually true. In fact, alcohol and other drug dependencies are often referred to as "the illnesses of denial." Although Kim's use of denial starts out like someone trying to deny some other serious illness, ***once she takes the first drink or other drug, she's in a whole different ballgame.*** Marijuana, alcohol, ecstasy, cocaine, etc., are mood-altering drugs. When someone drinks or uses enough to get high, ***their judgment is impaired. The way they perceive reality is chemically distorted.*** The use of defense mechanisms escalates. This is why the drug dependent person is usually the last one to know there is a problem.

Lynn: So, in other words, Kim doesn't see herself the way other people do.

Jim: Yes. The drug-dependent person, with his or her distorted thinking, often ***sees the consequences*** of drinking or using (school problems, family hassles, and trouble with the law) ***and perceives that these are the causes*** of the increased drinking or using. This may sound like "I smoke weed (or pot) because I like it." Someone doesn't use marijuana or alcohol when they are alone or in the morning because ***they like to.*** At that point they are drinking or using because ***they need to.***

Ed: Kim sometimes says to me: "If you didn't nag me so much, I wouldn't have to stay out so late." Then I get even angrier.

When Kim first started drinking and trying marijuana it might have been experimental or giving into peer pressure. Some teenagers, and some preteens, may initially use alcohol or other drugs to self-medicate undetected symptoms of depression, post traumatic stress disorder, or other conditions. Ongoing research suggests that heredity can also play a very significant role in increasing one's susceptibility to many illnesses, including alcoholism and other drug dependences. *[See chapter 5, "Why* My *Kid?"]*

Jim: Let's look at the progression of drug dependence a little closer. I'll illustrate for you what I mean by using a series of circles.

When a drug-dependent person first starts drinking or using other drugs, it's mostly fun and enjoyable. The "enjoyment" may also include the reduction of unpleasant feelings (shyness, loneliness, etc.) and/or painful feelings (anxiety, depression, memories of trauma, etc.). (Many recovering alcoholics and recovering drug-dependent people explain that when they first started drinking or using, they appeared to experience an even greater degree of physical and emotional pleasure than most other people.) Initially the little pain (if any) or trouble resulting from excessive use might be an occasional hangover or slight embarrassment for one's behavior.

Ed: That sounds like a number of adults I know. It has even happened to me a few times when I had too much to drink.

Jim: Sure Ed, in fact, it's probably impossible to tell the difference between a social drinker (adult), a drug experimenter, or an alcohol or drug-dependent person at that point. However, the problem, as time goes by, gets worse. The fun decreases and the PAIN or trouble increases. Alcohol and drugs just aren't working as well after awhile. They continue to interfere in one or more areas of the user's life. This PAIN might be social, (embarrassment, arguments), academic (grades, attendance, and behavior problems), emotional (mood swings, or guilt), physical, or legal.

Lynn: So why don't they just stop using or at least not do it often?

Jim: Because they can't!

Ed: What do you mean they can't? Kim has stopped before. She just doesn't seem to care.

Jim: By the very nature of their illness, ***alcohol and other drug-dependent individuals cannot*** **consistently** ***control their use, nor*** **consistently** ***predict what will happen when they do use. Ongoing recovery from alcohol or drug dependency begins with not taking the first drink or drug!*** As is sometimes said in Alcoholics Anonymous: "One drink (or drug) is too many and 20 is not enough."

Lynn: So that means if Kim were of legal drinking age, she couldn't drink again?

Jim: Yes, at least not in safety. This is one of the main reasons why the user tries to deny that his or her use is a problem. Denial, however, enables the illness to progress and get worse. This only causes ***MORE*** **PAIN.** As the pain begins to equal or exceed the fun or pleasure, the dependent person tries to "turn back the clock (see arrows)."

Lynn: What do you mean?

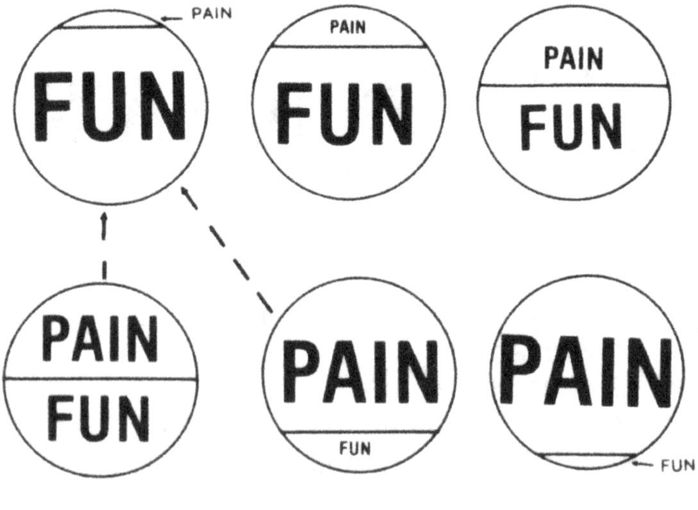

Jim: They try to return to the time when the drinking or using was mostly fun. They attempt to "control" their use by setting limits: "I'll only have two puffs on a joint," or, switching to beer, they might think: "You can't be an alcoholic if you only drink beer." (There is actually slightly more alcohol in a 12 ounce can of beer than there is in a four ounce glass of wine or one-ounce shot of whiskey or vodka.) [3] Or they may say: "If I use marijuana once in awhile what's the big deal?"

Ed: You are describing Kim.

Jim: Once someone begins to admit there is a problem in controlling their use, deep down inside they know they may have to stop using. The drug-dependent person increasingly tries to convince themselves that they can control their use or stop anytime they want to. To convince themselves that they are not addicted, they subconsciously use other defense mechanisms like minimizing "I never buy weed" or "I only had a hangover a few times," or rationalizing "I smoke weed because it relaxes me" or "I cut school because it's boring."

Lynn: Now you sound exactly like Kim! I am so frustrated. I do not know what else to do! I have tried everything I can think of to help her—pouring booze down the drain, cleaning up after her, and making excuses to others. I would do anything to keep her from getting into trouble!

Jim: Protecting the user from the consequences of their drinking or drugging is called enabling.

Although your instincts are normal, ***enabling the drug-dependent person backfires!*** Eventually, the user is unable to just "think" the problem away. **The *pain continues to get worse.*** Even drinking or drugging more cannot block out all of reality all of the time. At this point, they try to get rid of the pain and other consequences of their drinking or drugging. They may say things like "write a note to my teacher, I don't feel like going to school," "lend me some money, I promise I'll pay you back," (and she goes out and buys more marijuana) or "don't tell anyone how I dented the car. I could lose my license."

Ed: When Kim had a car accident well past her curfew, I covered for her and some of our friends thought I was the one who dented the car!

Lynn: I was so afraid she'd fail at school that I wrote a note saying she was sick when actually she was too hung-over to get to school on time. I hate myself when I lie for her!

Jim: As the alcohol or drug-dependent person tries to get rid of the pain, where do you suppose most of that pain goes?

Lynn: Ouch, to me! I have trouble eating and sleeping. I have even missed a lot of time from work because of it, and ***I am not the one who is using drugs!***

Jim: The pain that drug abusers experience is the direct result of the natural consequences of their behavior. This is what alcohol and drug abuse does to people. ***Pain, can be one of the main motivators for change.*** One of the definitions of the word ***"crisis" is "a turning point in the course of an illness." Can you begin to see by enabling Kim we feed right into her denial system?*** Who is it helping? Kim? Either of you? Anyone?

Lynn: It certainly isn't doing wonders for my own health or the rest of the family's. I wish I had learned about this sooner. Maybe she would have stopped by now.

Jim: What makes you think that you can make her stop using? Alcoholism and other drug dependencies are illnesses! It is not in your power to make her get clean and sober, no matter how much you love her. Has anything you've tried worked so far?

Lynn: I guess not, or else I wouldn't be here.

Ed: You're right! Sometimes I think I'm going out of my mind. One minute I want to throw her out of the house and the next minute I remember what a wonderful person she used to be and can be again.

Jim: You sound like you need to go to Al-Anon.

Ed: What is Al-Anon?

Jim: Al-Anon and Alateen (for teenagers) are support groups for people who are affected by someone else's drinking. Together they share their experiences, strength, and hope and learn more effective ways to cope with their problems.

Lynn: I would be uncomfortable going to an Al-Anon meeting. What would people think?

Jim: That you care about someone who has a problem with alcohol and at times other drugs—***just like them!*** There are many thousands of people who have felt the way you do now, and many have found help and hope in Al-Anon. First, by realizing ***we cannot make someone else stop drinking or using,*** we can begin to redirect our concern and energy in more constructive ways.

Ed: But if Kim would just stop using, everything would be OK.

Jim: Sure, things would be better if she stopped, but how do you suppose you would feel the next time she came home 15 minutes late?

Lynn: Oh God, I would be all uptight again, afraid she had gotten high!

Jim: **Preoccupation with the user's behavior causes pain!** ***Much of your painful feelings are the direct result of your preoccupation with her illness—whether she is using or not.***

The more we think about what the drinker or user is doing or might do, the more painful feelings we experience (worry, fear, guilt, anger, shame). As time goes by, our thoughts and feelings can become dominated by her illness. ***THIS IS OBSESSION.***

Jim: Do you like the way you feel?
Ed: No way!
Lynn: I certainly don't.
Jim: Then maybe it's time for each of you to decide if you want to change the way you feel, or do you want to continue to feel as if you are at the wrong end of an emotional YO YO string, with Kim's illness yanking you around?
Lynn: And going to these meetings can help with this … how to not worry so much that I can't even breathe?

Jim: Yes, involvement in support groups like Al-Anon and Nar-Anon (support groups for people affected by someone else's drug use) can really help! There are people who have had most of the same feelings and struggles as you and they have found that by attending these meetings, they were able to get a better perspective on their own situation. We may not like the fact that someone we love is sick. We do not have to like it! However, ***as we change our own attitudes, reactions, and feelings, our lives do become more manageable.*** This often also has a positive effect in our relationships with all of our children, including the drug-dependent person. This can also significantly improve the chances of the drinker or user accepting help sooner or to increase the chances of them remaining alcohol and drug free!

Over the next several weeks, Jim continues to meet with Kim once a week and, periodically in family sessions. She is resistant to attend AA or NA, stating, "I'm not that bad" and "I'm not like those burnt-out people." Her parents are trying to continue to learn more about alcohol and drug dependence in order to gain more insight into the effect it has had on their lives. They also continue to learn how to redirect their energy in more effective ways to help Kim and themselves.

Lynn: As you suggested, we went to a couple of Al-Anon meetings.

Ed: I can see how it might be possible for some people to detach from a husband or wife who is the drinker or drug abuser, but ***how do you detach from a sixteen-year-old?***

Lynn: This is ***my*** little girl—how can I just abandon her and turn my back on her?

Jim: ***Detaching does not mean not caring.*** Detaching is redirecting your love and energy in more helpful ways for all of you. As we learn to detach, we learn not to suffer so much because someone we love is struggling. How can you help Kim when her illness is doing such a job on you?

Ed: I know we have talked about that before. I've lost enough sleep already. Sometimes I get so angry it just makes things worse. It seems like Kim and I just "lock horns" together.

Lynn: One thing I noticed at the last Al-Anon meeting I went to was the hope I saw in many of the faces.

Ed: Yeah. I did feel better being there with people who had similar problems, but I'm not sure why.

Jim: Ed, did you notice the hope in the other people as Lynn did?

Ed: Maybe it was hope I saw, but how can I sleep at night knowing that if she goes back to using, she could get arrested or suspended from school or worse?

Jim: Ed, can you hear yourself still denying the fact that Kim, with her parents help, is responsible for her own choices and recovery, and that no matter how much you worry, you cannot make her stay clean and sober? As you continue to try to accept this, hope will grow. Hope is a result of taking ***action.***

Ed: What kind of action?

Jim: Continuing what you are already doing.

Lynn: You mean keep going to meetings?

Jim: You got it! *[All three laugh.]* The difficulties you are experiencing are normal. You are only human. You are already admitting the seriousness of the situation: accepting takes more time. And it takes help—the help of people coming together and sharing their strength, hope, and experience. By being actively involved in support group such as Al-Anon, people also gain a lot of valuable day-to-day experience in coping with serious illness. ***If you find something helpful, keep at it.*** Remember, however, that we are dealing with an ***illness*** and not just behavioral problems. Our number-one recommendation to parents is that they become and stay actively involved in support groups such as Al-Anon [4], Nar-Anon [5], and or Families Anonymous [6] because they are specifically designed to help people who are affected by someone else's drinking or drugging. ***Al-Anon, with more than 26,000 groups in 115 countries throughout the world, helps more families of alcoholics than any other single resource.***

Chapter 2

UNDERSTANDING AND COPING WITH CHRONIC DISEASE

Probably the most important thing for parents to understand, in order to be more effective in helping their son or daughter, is that ***alcohol and other drug dependencies are illnesses!*** In many ways, coping with alcohol and other drug dependencies is similar to other chronic illness.

We have selected diabetes as another example of a chronic illness to help illustrate similarities between treatment and response. Both diabetes and alcohol and drug dependencies ***are treatable*** but currently not curable. By this we mean they cannot be surgically removed or eliminated by a medication. Once an alcoholic (or drug-dependent), always an alcoholic. Once a diabetic, always a diabetic. However, ***in the majority of cases, people with either illness can learn about their disease, get help, and learn how to maintain recovery "One Day At a Time."***

The more a person learns about their illness and how to arrest it (for the diabetic---how to maintain a healthy blood sugar level; alcohol and or drug-dependent—how to live clean and sober), the more ***freedom*** it gives them in their daily lives—***freedom to live life*** with fewer restrictions due to the illness. Learning about someone else's illness, what you can and cannot do to help him or her as well as how to help yourself, can also give family members more

freedom from blaming themselves for the illness, more ***freedom from isolation, fear, and distress.***

One of the differences between these illnesses is that ***alcohol and other drug dependencies are the only illnesses we know of where we expect those with the illness to diagnose it themselves and to instinctively know what needs to be done in order to get better.***

Remember the drug-dependent person has not learned yet that he or she is sick and that drinking and drugging is the cause of their problems or making pre-existing problems worse. This is the only illness where we expect the family to be able to diagnose the illness and automatically know what to do next! It is also an illness that probably has more myths, misconceptions, and misdiagnoses than any other illness. *THIS DOES NOT HAVE TO BE!*

A large proportion of professionals, including both authors of this book, were initially trained to look at parenting styles as the main contributor to problems with children and adolescents. Over time, as a result of what we have learned from doing research of our own as well as what we have learned from working with many parents, we continue to evolve our counseling approach to consider a wide variety of factors. We have broadened our approach to understanding how parents of alcohol and drug-dependent adolescents are affected by their son's or daughter's disease by reading about how parents respond to many other acute and chronic illnesses and conditions affecting teens. We developed the

Parental Distress Response Survey as a means of demonstrating these similarities.

Following is a series of statements or quotes about a parent's response to a particular severe illness of a son or a daughter. What illness is each of these comments referring to? (See the end of this chapter for the answers.)

1. "It was a long time before I could say that sometimes I hate her for all the problems she presents. I often feel as if I am bled dry."
2. "As a parent, you may blame yourself for her illness or for not having noticed it earlier."
3. "You might feel angry at yourself, your spouse, your child, the doctor who gave you the diagnosis, or even God. But what you're really angry at is...."
4. "I'm going crazy. People treat me like I'm a bad parent. I feel violated."
5. "Disappointment that a child is not perfect poses a threat to many parents' egos and a challenge to their value system."

Parental or family distress is a condition where an individual or family's resources can be stretched beyond apparent limits. These resources may include emotional and physical endurance, finances, and social supports. When people are overwhelmed, their ability to respond effectively is often diminished. "Parental Distress Response," Richard P. DeSantis, PhD, Gerald J. Manney, MS, *Adolescence Magazine,* January 1994.

Feeling guilt for their child's disease may be more of a normal response to dealing with acute and/or chronic child or adolescent onset diseases. Guilt, while being initially overwhelming, may serve temporarily as a coping devise. "If I am to blame; if I change, then maybe my son or daughter will be all right ... but if it is a disease then—oh my God—maybe I can't fix it." As with many things in life, too much or too little of something can cause problems. "An appropriate sense of guilt makes people try to be better. But an excessive sense of guilt, a tendency to blame ourselves for things which are clearly not our fault, robs us of our self-esteem and perhaps our capacity to grow and act." [7] Too much guilt can consume precious time and energy as well as divert us from changing the things we *can* change.

The following is from the article "Just for Parents" on the American Diabetes Association Web site:
"Did she get diabetes from my side of the family?"
"I should have recognized that something was wrong sooner that I did."
"Does he have diabetes now because I didn't cook well enough for him before?"
"Harboring this kind of guilt doesn't do anyone any good. The truth is that no one knows why certain people get diabetes and others don't."

The chart on the following page provides a comparison of some of the similarities of alcohol and other drug dependencies and another more socially accepted chronic illness: diabetes.

	Physical	Psychological	Behavioral
Characteristics	Chronic Can be treated and arrested but is currently not curable Large percent of population is affected Heredity increases the risk of developing the disease	Initial denial of illness Feelings of: Anger Confusion Guilt Fear Depression Mood swings Disease affects family Acceptance of illness is difficult	Adjustments to chronic disease are necessary Inconsistent treatment results in more frequent life problems Individual and family reactions to the illness
Treatment	Consistent regimen is needed Daily self-assessment and care Sufficient rest and sleep are necessary Maintain healthy diet	Overcoming fear of treatment Understanding and accepting the existence of the illness and its chronic nature Understanding and accepting of own feelings Understanding mood swings May utilize support available such as self-help groups, family, friends, and faith	Learning about the illness is critical Myths and misconceptions complicate treatment Living a day at a time Individual and family readjustment to changes Adolescent onset disease necessitates shared responsibility for recovery
Relapse	Inconsistent application of treatment Initial treatment provided may have been inadequate Available research on relapse is incomplete	Continued denial of seriousness of the illness Inadequate commitment to recovery Difficulty in resisting peer pressure Complacency	Testing of the illness severity Inadequate use of support systems Following inappropriate role models Insufficient vigilance

Let's return to a meeting with our parents as other feelings come to the surface:

Lynn: A lot of this information and going to Al-Anon has been very helpful in starting to understand what's going on with Kim and us. **But, *if I had known sooner what the real problem was—if only I had done something sooner … maybe things would have been different!***

Ed: [*Nods in agreement.*]

Jim: You sound angry and frustrated.

Lynn: You're damn right I am! And the more I think about it, the madder I get!

Jim: Does it do anyone any good to hold onto the past—what might have been?

Lynn: I don't like feeling angry all of the time.

Jim: You didn't answer my question.

Lynn: No, but I don't know how to let go of it.

Ed: Yeah, it tears me up also! I usually just stuff it and try to put it out of my mind.

Jim: Have either of you flown on a commercial airliner?

Lynn: Yes. We have on a number of occasions.

Jim: Do you remember the instructions the flight attendant gave before the plane took off? If the cabin pressure drops oxygen masks will automatically fall. If you are with a child or infant, whom should you give the oxygen to first, the child or yourself?

Lynn: Yourself … because if you should pass out from lack of oxygen, how can you help the child?

Ed: I need to remember that if I don't help myself, I am not going to be able to help anyone else.

Jim: Maybe things might have been different had you sought help sooner, and maybe they wouldn't have. You did the best you could. ***Remember, this is a powerful illness we are dealing with. You are not imagining things. This is difficult! Many people find it helpful to remember the four C's. I didn't* CAUSE *it. I can't* CURE *it. I can't* CONTROL *it.*** *But* ***I can learn to* COPE *with it.*** Dwelling on the past only makes us feel worse, wastes valuable energy, and interferes with our ability to change what we can. But ***with help you can meet the challenges head on.*** Most professionals involved with the treatment of alcohol and other drug dependencies agree that informed families significantly increase the chances of recovery. Once again, one of the best ways to redirect your energy in more effective ways for yourselves, and for Kim, is to continue what you are doing—getting help for yourself.

Lynn: A friend of mine, who is not in Al-Anon, writes her thoughts and feelings in a journal. I wonder if that would be helpful to me.

Jim: There are many tools and skills that people find helps them reduce stress and strain, including "journalizing," stress-management techniques, meditation, moderate exercise, walking, or going to a movie. When was the last time either of you did something just for fun?

Lynn: I'm so busy talking care of everyone that I hardly ever think about me. No wonder I feel like such a wreck.

Ed: I don't trust Kim to be alone in our house without one of us there, and when I try to do something with one of my friends my mind is usually thinking about what's going on at home. It's like I'm damned if I do and damned if I don't.

Jim: Taking "One Thing At a Time" and "One Step At a Time" can either of you think of any ways that you can do something to enjoy yourselves that wouldn't be so stressful?

Lynn: Ed, what if we invited our friends Tom and Mary over some night for dessert?

Ed: That seems like a good idea. I just thought of something I heard at one of the Al-Anon meetings we went to: "KISS," Keep It Simple Sweetheart. Tom and Mary don't have a problem with alcohol or drugs in the family, but they know about Kim and are fun to be with.

The following is taken from the “Suggested Opening” read at the beginning of an Al-Anon meeting. “As we learn to place our problem in their true perspective, we find it loses its power to dominate our thoughts and our lives. The family situation is bound to improve as we apply the Al-Anon principles.” In continuing to put the focus on ourselves, **we find more things that we can do to reduce our stress and help bring more stability to our daily lives,** despite dealing with alcohol or drug dependence or other chronic illnesses.

When was the last time you have been to your primary care physician for a checkup? Have you told your doctor about your son’s or daughter’s problem? Excessive stress can be creating or aggravating your own health issues. It can also cover up other symptoms or distract you from getting help with other medical issues not related to the stress in your life.

In gathering information for this book, the authors polled many parents. When asked, “What suggestions, tools, etc., have been most helpful to you in coping with your son’s or daughter’s alcohol or drug dependency,” the most common response was: “My participation in Al-Anon.” Many parents also found similar support groups, counseling, and other resources to be helpful.

Support groups for patients and families exist for many other illnesses, including diabetes, cancer, and congenital heart disease. What most people don’t know is that AA, [8] an organization started in 1935, is the oldest ongoing self-help group for people with an illness and that Al-Anon, founded in 1951, is the oldest self-help group for families. There are currently more than 400 self-help and support groups, many modeled after AA, for various illnesses and problems.[9]

Answers to the Family Distress Response Survey.

1. Cerebral Palsy, The Resilient Family, Power, Paul W., ScD. Dell Orto, PhD, Sorin Books, Notre Dame, Indiana, 2003.
2. Diabetes, Living with Diabetes http://www.diabetes.org.
3. Diabetes, American Diabetes Association, Just for Parents, 2003.
4. Marijuana Dependence, father of a 16-year-old son.
5. Head Injury, Lezak, Muriel, PhD, "Brain Damage Is a Family Affair," *Journal of Clinical and Experimental Neuropsychology,* Vol. 10. 1988.

PART II

SUPPORTING RECOVERY

Chapter 3

SHARED RESPONSIBILITY AND SETTING EXAMPLES

In many ways, recovery from adult-onset alcohol or drug dependence is similar to recovery from adolescent-onset dependence. That is, if you admit you have a problem and can't deal with it alone, take responsibility for getting better, get help (counseling, AA, and/or NA meetings), and don't take the first drink or drug. One of the ways that adolescent-onset alcohol or drug dependence differs from adult-onset dependence is the shared responsibility for recovery.

Responsibility for recovery from any illness essentially rests on the shoulders of the adolescent or adult who has the illness. That is, if you are not able to "fix it" yourself, you need to seek appropriate help and follow all the necessary steps to get better and/or prevent the illness from getting worse. Teenagers however, don't have the mental and emotional maturity, coping skills, or life experience (even though they may think they do) for effective, sustained independent living, let alone dealing with a serious illness by themselves. This is why they need parents. *(Also see chapter 5, Setting Limits.)* Younger children are more or entirely dependent upon adults to deal with any illness).

Alcohol and other drug abuse distort judgment. Repeated abuse of alcohol or drugs can also result in ongoing cognitive (thinking) impairments that can take days, weeks, or months to remedy. ***The main part of the body that becomes disrupted by repeated***

abuse of alcohol and other drugs is the brain. It is also the organ that is needed to learn how to recover from alcohol or drug dependence and live clean and sober.

Sixteen-year-old David R. poignantly illustrates this point in a letter he wrote to other teenagers who were getting help for their drug problems.

> The other day, while I was fishing with my father and aunt, we came across a giant sea turtle with a lobster pot line wrapped around one of its fins. The huge animal was floundering helplessly in the water. If it was not promptly freed, it would surely have died. With the aid of my dad and aunt, I managed to uncoil the noose binding its fin. Although the turtle was crashing around violently in the water and trying to swim away in fear, we saved it.
>
> I wanted to share this experience with you, because I recognized the similarities between that turtle and me, and how it took the help of treatment, AA, and my family to free me from the fatal grip of drugs and alcohol. I could not do it myself, as the turtle could not free its fin from the line by itself. When someone tried to help me with it, I resisted violently ... It's (recovery) a long, hard, and slow process, but it's well worth it. Believe me, I know ... I feel better about myself. I feel healthier in both mind and body, more so than I have in years.

Informed parental involvement in the treatment of adolescent-onset alcohol and other drug dependencies, as in the treatment of adolescent-onset diabetes and other serious illnesses is vital. An adolescent doesn't have the life experiences, maturity, or coping skills for effective, sustained, independent living. This is why they need parents or other caregivers. Although one is legally an adult at age 18, many young people are not mentally or emotionally mature enough to be fully self-supporting.

Shared Responsibility for Recovery		
Includes	**Need Not Include**	**Probably Should Not Include**
Attending counseling and/or AA or NA (for parents Al-Anon and or similar supports)	Taking responsibility for the illness itself	Protecting (within reason) the teen from the natural consequences of their behaviors
Keeping counseling appointments	How much teen learns from his or her own experience	Punishing yourself for their illness
Learning about alcohol and drug dependence	Suffering when teen has a relapse	Bailing him or her out of jail (you may want to seek specific advice of a lawyer on this issue)
Learning the language of recovery, "One Day At a Time," "Easy Does It," "First Things First"		
Possibly driving son or daughter to counseling, AA, and or NA		
Following through in getting help whether the teen does or not		
Setting healthy examples		
Parents and teen may both contribute to the cost of professional treatment		

SETTING EXAMPLES

It is important to note that the parents' example will, to some extent, be modeled by the teen. It is important to try to present a positive example that can help influence him or her. Alcoholism and other drug dependencies are illnesses, for which people need help (parents too).

Positive examples can help communicate that:

1. It is all right to get help. Everyone needs help sometimes.
2. ***This is serious***. So serious that we are taking significant steps; we regularly attend Al-Anon and/or Nar-Anon, and/or counseling, and we are continuing to learn as much as we can.
3. We care! We care enough to ***do*** something about it.
4. We believe you are a good person whose illness can result in you doing bad or hurtful things.

Our attitudes, actions, and tone of voice can also communicate and help perpetuate many of the stereotypes and misconceptions about alcoholism or drug dependence. Coping with a major disease is hard enough. Being stigmatized exaggerates the situation. Perhaps the most potentially harmful effect of all of this is that it diverts precious energy and time from receiving treatment. ***Without appropriate treatment any serious treatment will usually get worse. Alcoholism and other drug dependencies are no exceptions.***

The inability or unwillingness of parents to follow through with help for themselves can communicate to the adolescent:

1. You are not sick and do not need help (like "real" alcoholics or drug addicts do).
2. It will go away. It's just a phase.
3. It's someone else's fault. If people, places, and things would change, we'd all be okay.
4. You are a bad person and deserve whatever you get.
5. You just have a bad habit. Use more willpower!

If it is hard for you to understand and accept drug dependence as an illness, you are like most people. Keep trying. If you find it difficult and frustrating to cope with, it is because you are human. You are not imagining things. ***This is difficult! But if you remember one thing—that you don't have to deal with this alone—you will be alright!***

You may have thought and felt this way at times; but if you were really convinced that the alcohol or drug-dependent person could just stop if they wanted to, you probably wouldn't be reading this. Just as your ***wishful thinking, denial, avoidance, and blaming can't block out reality all of the time, the same is true for the drug-dependent person.*** Remember when you waited for your son or daughter to change; remember when you got **sick and tired** of feeling sick and tired? Good. Let's keep up the good work (you are really helping yourself and your teen—even if you can't always see the immediate effects).

Our characters, Jim, Ed, and Lynn may give us some insight into this. Let's hear more from them.

Lynn: Sometimes I just don't know if anything I do makes any difference anymore.

Jim: What you do does matter! Even if you could turn back the clock and be the perfect parent *[in over 30 years of counseling, I've never met a perfect parent. I certainly wasn't myself* (Jerry).*]* Kim may still have gotten into trouble with alcohol and other drugs. Remember, Ed and Lynn, you now ***know*** it's a disease, that Kim is a sick person whose illness can make her do bad things.

Ed: You're absolutely right! I am trying to accept that.

Lynn: I want to believe that, and I am slowly learning how. I am also feeling that way more and more.

Ed: I love my daughter *[fighting back tears,]* but I hate her disease!

Jim: You're doing alright, folks. Remember you are only human. This is also the only disease in which families, especially parents, are unrealistically expected to diagnose their adolescent's illness (often before we professionals do) and somehow instinctively know what to do about it. I think it is important to emphasize that you are good parents of a sick kid, not bad parents of a spoiled delinquent. You didn't know how serious things were and maybe were also afraid to know … but now you do know and are doing something constructive about it. The goodness, caring, and sensitivity we see, at times, in Kim is a re-emergence of the "real Kim." It didn't just happen in her; the two of you had a lot to do with it.

Ed: Thank you. Sometimes I just need to hear that ***again and again!***

Lynn: ***And again!*** *[All three laugh.]* That's one of the ways Al-Anon has helped me the most. No matter how much I learn, sometimes I need to hear other people say: "You're doing all right, Lynn. You're making progress."

Jim: Consider this. As difficult as all of this is for you as parents to cope with, think how difficult it must be for a young person to cope with his or her own disease. **Teens not only lack the years of experience adults have, but *also parts of the brain that we use to learn from our experience continue to physically develop until about age 20*.** This is another reason why teens need parents', or other guardians' support and guidance. *[This will be discussed more in chapter 4, "Setting Limits."]*

As the three continued to talk, another issue came up: "Should we serve alcohol to our friends in our home and should we even have alcohol in our home?" There is no one set answer to this frequently asked question. Parents who use alcohol responsibly shouldn't feel the need or obligation to abstain from drinking any more than they would stop eating some foods if their child were diagnosed as having diabetes. It is also important, however, to consider that the teen may have strong feelings about this and is entitled to share his or her views.

Many alcoholics answer: “It doesn’t matter to me. If I want to drink, I’ll get it somehow.” If you don’t serve alcohol to our guests because of me, I know (and they probably know) that the only reason is because of me, and I don’t like that.” Some family members may not feel comfortable having a drink in front of the teen for a while and may choose not to drink in their presence during his or her early recovery.

It is difficult to list “do’s” and “don’ts” for all people and all situations. Neither this book nor any other book alone can provide a specific blueprint for all parents to follow. This is why continued parental involvement in Al-Anon, Nar-Anon, and/or counseling is so important. As family members continue to learn about the disease and how they have been affected by someone else’s drinking or using, they can discover more options and learn additional skills. These—combined with an open mind, love, and common sense—will help them adapt to their own situation.

Chapter 4

SETTING LIMITS

When parents feel frustrated about inappropriate behaviors, they may tend to want to establish a "stranglehold" on the teen's behavior in an attempt to force change. This often results in more frequent, as well as more intense, conflicts between parent and teen and can easily contribute to a parent(s) becoming very distressed and burned-out. Some parents, feeling overwhelmed or worn down by the teen's continued badgering and/or whining, may bend the rules so often that it appears there are few or any rules at all. Both approaches can contribute to the problems and not the solutions. Parents, in an attempt to prevent angry outbursts by the teen, may even find themselves "walking on eggshells," afraid to say the wrong thing or do the wrong thing. Trying harder to help your son or daughter may not be possible and may also be adding to frustration and burnout. Instead, redirecting our concern in more effective ways, can lead parents to use opportunities for change in helping their teen while also conserving their precious and limited energy.

Teenagers, whether they have an alcohol or a drug problem or not, ***need parents or guardians.*** (It is not uncommon for children and teenagers to live with their grandparents, often due to severe alcoholism or other drug dependence in one or both parents. There are also many single parents who may have varying degrees of support, or lack of support, from the other parent.)

It is important to remember that limits merely serve as guidelines. ***Guidelines are not meant to be blueprints from which there is no deviation.*** A guideline can be described as a rope or cord that serves to direct one's steps. It is not an umbilical cord in which a teen is totally dependent on a parent. Neither is it a lariat to lasso someone (although we may be tempted to), tie them up, and prevent them from making mistakes. Parents, by action, example, and love, help shape their child's maturity. They do not control it. Completely ***controlling a child's or teenager's behavior at any age is a myth.*** Limits may also serve as a boundary, a passageway within the borders of safe action, appropriate social interaction, and acceptable and unacceptable behavior. Parents, through their own experiences and from experience of others (Al-Anon, Nar-Anon, family, friends, and community supports), continue to learn to adapt limit setting to their own situations. Our characters discuss this further.

Lynn: When I first began to face Kim's drug dependence, I didn't realize how much it would force me to grow and change. With help and time, I think I have become more consistent with Kim.

Jim: In what ways, Lynn?

Lynn: I have learned to listen before I react and think through my decisions, and I am usually aware that I need to be consistent with earlier decisions I have made. The other day Kim asked for the use of the car, even though she knew she had been grounded for two weeks. I was tempted to let her but I decided to be patient and consistent with our earlier agreement that she could not use the car for a set amount of time. And I think being more consistent has helped me become more patient with her.

Jim: Often by stopping and thinking first instead of yelling and threatening when we get angry, we are more able to follow through on our decisions or statements. ***Children and teens need rules and structure, even though at times they may dislike them***. Being consistent means continuing to "adhere," or stick to, the same principles or course of action, without frequently giving in or being self-contradictory. Letting our kids get us on a guilt-trip, feeling sorry for our children, overreacting when we are angry, and feeling very tired or worn-out ***are some of the more common reasons parents report that lead them to give in to the child or teen's*** **wants** ***instead of responding to their*** **needs.** Occasionally changing our mind or even caving in to a teen's request does not necessarily mean parents are being inconsistent. Instead these may be examples of modeling to our children that it is OK to rethink a decision and change one's mind. It also shows that we make mistakes, try to learn from them and are, in fact, human.

Repeating yourself more than once or twice often has the backward effect of training the child to wait for repeated statements or warnings before they respond. It is also one of the main ways they try to wear you down. Children and teens want what they want, when they want it. They usually have the energy to continue to hound you until you give into their wishes. Even if you give in to their pestering one out of four times, they seem to remember the time they were able to wear you down and get what they wanted. ***Continuing to repeat instructions to your son or daughter or arguing with him or her until you finally lose your temper can also feed right into their defense mechanisms.*** We often hear rationalizations like "That's it. I'm out of here! There's nothing wrong with me … my only problem is having you for a parent."

Ed: ***"Say what you mean, mean what you say, without saying it mean."***

Jim: Hey, I like that one.

Ed: I heard it at a meeting last week. Someone there said that if he isn't able to do all three of those, he tries to postpone a decision until he's had a chance to calm down, think the issue through, and maybe talk to another person in Al-Anon. I have been picking up a lot of helpful things like that. Another thing I've learned is that it is important to be realistic about when I expect Kim to be able to do something, and how well I expect her to do it. I can now see that in the first few weeks after she stopped drinking and smoking marijuana, often it was all she could do to attend school, go to counseling and meetings, and stay clean and sober. *[Kim finds attending both AA and NA* *helpful.]* She wasn't able to do all the things I wanted "my little girl" to do. She was not going to be able to handle all of my expectations like cleaning and organizing her room, getting a part-time job, changing her circle of friends, and so on. [*These expectations may vary from parent to parent and teen to teen.]*

Jim: As Kim begins to admit she has a problem and becomes increasingly responsible for following through with her own treatment, other issues, such as chores, can be discussed one at a time. A very important part of her recovery process is physical. Research studies suggest that ***repeated abuse of alcohol and other drugs, including marijuana, disrupt parts of brain functioning even for a period of time after someone has stopped drinking or using.*** Some of the areas that appear to be affected deal with concentration, short-term memory, mood swings, and abstract reasoning. These impairments will usually be corrected by significant periods of abstinence and proper nutrition, but healing also takes time ... more time than either you or Kim like.

Lynn: Oh God, I feel like I need to go to another Al-Anon meeting.

Ed: I remember when our neighbor fell off a ladder. After he left the hospital, it took months of physical therapy before he could get around. I suppose it is similar in some ways to Kim's recovery.

Lynn: I need to keep reminding myself how Kim might feel. After all, ***she's the one with the illness.***

Jim: Often an adolescent's "attitude" isn't about us, but instead may be an expression of their frustrations, fears, and insecurities. As challenging as this can be for parents, it may be an example that she feels safe to let her guard down at home instead of trying to continue to project an outwardly "cool" image as adolescents often do when they are around their peers.

Ed: I hadn't thought that the way I was reacting some of the time was not ever fair. I wasn't ready to allow Kim to have any input into setting some of these limits.

Jim: How much input do you think Kim has been given in this?

Lynn: Well, you have been seeing Kim individually in counseling; what does she say?

Jim: I can't answer that because my conversations with her are confidential, just as ours are here today.

Ed: I guess I would have to think about your question, Jim.

Lynn: I have noticed I tend to discuss things more openly and try to get her side of the issue before I make a decision.

People overwhelmed by a problem often see only two alternatives: do everything ... or do nothing. When one is considering setting more limits on a teen's behavior, it often starts with thoughts like "That's it, I've had it! I won't take any more garbage from this kid! I'm finally going to lay the law down! Things better change and change now!" At times, friends or relatives may say to you "Kick him or her out of the house if they drink or use again." Idle threats don't appear to have much of an impact on the drinker or user. Kicking a teen, who is younger than 18, out of the house, can result in legal problems for the parents. Many parents of a son or daughter who is 18 or over report feeling more worried about them *after* they have left the house.

It's not uncommon to feel an extreme level of frustration and aggravation now and then, but it's usually better to ***stop and think before you react.*** It may be more constructive to postpone certain decisions for a while until we are more able to explore options as well as to better understand our own motivations. *Are we acting* in an attempt to guide and support the teen toward positive changes and/or to protect ourselves and the other children from the drinker or user's unacceptable behavior, or *are we reacting* and slipping backward into the trap of thinking that "By God I'm going to *make that kid stop*" drinking and using?"

Remember, ***what is causing your frustration, pain, and heartache is the behavior resulting from her illness, not the teen,*** so our responses need to be more balanced. Balance includes responding to the drug-dependent teenager as an individual. Limits we place on a 13-year-old will differ to some degree from those expected of a 17-year-old, whether they have been abusing drugs or not. When we are angry, we may find ourselves giving the teen a consequence that later on we think too harsh.

Lynn: When I'm angry sometimes I feel like grounding her until she is 30! Well, maybe not that long, but I do find that I am more likely to set an unrealistic consequence and then later on, out of guilt, give in and let Kim off the hook.

Jim: I can't prove it, but I think kids can smell guilt in a parent from the time they are very young.

Ed: Oh yeah, I know what you mean! I can see it when Lynn and Kim interact, but it's so much harder for me to see when I'm overreacting. I think I'm more able to see things in myself when I hear others share at an Al-Anon meeting. When I am at a meeting, I find myself being calmer and more objective, but when I am at home and I hear Lynn and Kim arguing, I want to jump in and fix things. Then it seems that we all get angrier, and I feel like I'm going crazy. I then tend to say things like "you are grounded until you change your attitude," and then we argue about that. Looking back, I can see that giving that kind of a consequence is a lose-lose situation. I have noticed if I wait until I am calmer, Lynn and I can talk about it and then often present a more united front when dealing with our daughter. I am also trying to practice some of the things I hear at meetings when I talk with Lynn, like reminding myself to "Stop and Think," "Easy Does It," "How Important Is It?" "Don't Go to Every Argument You Are Invited to," and….

Lynn: OK. OK. I think he gets the point! Sometimes it helps me to see some humor in the situation, kind of a dark humor that lessens the stress.

As human beings we can only control 50 percent of any discussion … what and* how *we respond. Another element of setting limits is acknowledging those things that are already being accomplished. Our preoccupation with someone else's alcohol or drug use often diverts attention from the positive things being done.

Jim: Are there some good qualities you see in Kim?

Ed: Of course there are. She's our daughter.

Jim: Can you give me an example?

Ed: I think she's talented in some ways; she often has a quick sense of humor, and when she's not high she can be very caring.

Lynn: This conversation is making me think that perhaps I'm not complementing Kim enough when she deserves it.

Ed: I was very proud of her when she admitted she had a problem. That must have been very difficult.

Jim: Have you told Kim that?

Ed: Well I, … *[hesitates.]*

Jim: Have you told Kim you're proud of her?

Ed: No, I guess I haven't. It's always been hard for me to put how I feel into words; and the longer I wait to say it, the harder it gets.

Jim: Your ability to recognize that and say it is progress. Keep talking about it with your Al-Anon friends and, little by little, try telling Kim how you feel.

Lynn: Ed had tears in his eyes when she gave him a Father's Day card. I know he loves her so very much. Ed and I have been able to talk more calmly to each other about how we feel. I see a number of things slowly changing for the better. However, I still have a difficult time knowing how much input to let Kim have in deciding where the limits should begin and end.

Jim: There are some things that can be negotiated and others that don't have to be. What do each of you consider to be non-negotiable?

Lynn: No drinking or using other drugs.

Ed: No one outside of the family is allowed in our home unless one of us is present.

Jim: Are there some things that you consider to be negotiable?

Lynn: Some weekend activities, chores around the house, and, maybe later on, some curfews.

Ed: I am willing to negotiate almost anything except Kim staying off alcohol and drugs.

Jim: The very nature of the illness of alcohol or drug dependence dictates some of these limits. **The fundamental non-negotiable limit for recovering drug- dependent people, of any age, is *any* use of alcohol or any other mood-*altering* drug at any *time.*** Parents have the right to declare that any use of drugs or drinking is unacceptable. This in not trying to control behavior, but rather exercising parental responsibility. ***Parental responsibility involves setting appropriate limits.***

In the more than 150 Parent Programs (ranging from four to 12 hours of educational discussion groups) I (Jerry) have facilitated ... the most frequent struggles parents have reported were curfews, school (attendance, grades, and behavior), associating with alcohol drug using friends, about use of the family car, being on probation, and other house rules. The parents would then list their issues according to what appeared to be directly enforceable, not directly enforceable, negotiable, and non-negotiable.

DIRECTLY ENFORCEABLE	**NOT DIRECTLY ENFORCEABLE**
Allowance	Attitude
Earning money by doing extra chores	Curfews
Use of the car	Drinking and/or using
Use of the computer and/or Internet	Peers
	School:
	Attendance
	Behavior
	Grades

(These may vary from parent to parent.)

NEGOTIABLE	**NON-NEGOTIABLE**
Allowance	Drinking and/or using
Curfews	School
Earning money by doing extra chores	Attendance
Use of the Car	Behavior
Use of the computer and/or Internet	Grades

The issues listed above are illustrated to help expand one's view of influencing vs. attempting to control a teen's behaviors. What is negotiable or non-negotiable is up to you, *as well as* **when** *you are willing and able to have those discussions.* Negotiating, by allowing the teen to have input on certain issues, may help to improve communication between the teen and parent or guardian, increase the teen's self-esteem, and increase their commitment to follow through on the desired action, or accept an agreed upon consequence(s). Another "trap" that some parents fall into is setting "open-ended consequences" such as "you can't use the car until you change your attitude" or "you are grounded until you stop drinking and using (and the teen gets high on the way to school, in school, or on the way home from school). These types of consequences can result in increasing conflicts while also decreasing the teen's motivation or incentive for positive changes. As one parent stated: "There is nothing left (privileges) to take away from my son."

As we added items to the list of ***NOT DIRECTLY ENFORCEABLE*** issues, parents would often express more frustration.

Ed: AUGHHHHH!!!!!

Jim: Remember, folks, what we are trying to do. Are we buying into the myth of thinking we can control someone else's behavior or are we ***focusing on what we* can *do?***

Lynn: It is so easy to fall into that trap, but I keep trying to catch myself, and it makes a difference.

Jim: Good for you. I can't tell parents how to get more energy to deal with everything, but together we can strategize on how to ***redirect your energy in more constructive*** **ways.** Parents can often waste precious time and energy by trying harder and harder to force a solution. ***When you feel as if you are banging your head up against a wall, you probably are! This may not be the time to try harder but, rather to try doing some things*** **differently.**

Ed: Boy, can I relate to that! Growing up as a kid I was always told: "If at first you don't succeed, try, try again." Sometimes when I keep trying harder and harder, it's almost like I get tunnel vision. I keep trying and trying until I succeed or blow up out of frustration and aggravation. I often can't even think of trying something different at the time. At a lot of the Al-Anon meetings I've been to I have heard people talk about using "The Serenity Prayer":

GOD, GRANT ME THE SERENITY
TO ACCEPT THE THINGS I CANNOT CHANGE,
COURAGE TO CHANGE THE THINGS I CAN,
AND WISDOM TO KNOW THE DIFFERENCE.

I wish I could remember to use it—***before*** a situation happens—instead of remembering afterward when it's too late.

Jim: ***You are not imaging things. This is difficult. You are not discussing some theoretical exercise. You are talking about your***

daughter's drug problem. At times you may need to repeat "The Serenity Prayer" or other slogans and reminders over and over before your mind stops racing. Taking "One Step At A Time", we may ask ourselves: "What can I do about this issue?," "How important Is this?," or "What am I just banging my head against the wall over?" Eventually we find that ***we do become able to catch ourselves sooner and sooner, and redirect our thoughts and actions in more constructive ways.***

Ed: I heard someone at a meeting say that when they are really frustrated they sometimes say: "God, Grant Me The Serenity"—***and do it now!*** *[Ed laughs.]*

Jim: How does it feel to laugh?

Ed: It feels real good! When I first went to Al-Anon, I used to think people were crazy when I would hear them laugh. Now I understand that we need to laugh sometimes or we will feel like we are going crazy.

Jim: We counselors frequently encourage family members to talk more to each other about their feelings and opinions. ***There are times, however, when it may be better not to talk,*** but rather to try to avoid continued escalation of anger and frustration by ***calling a "time-out.*** "This is different from the time-outs that parents may use with a small child to help him or her become less agitated and learn to modulate their feelings. At a calm, or relatively calm moment, discuss the ground rules for a time-out. Anyone can call a "time-out" if he or she feels that they are about to lose their temper and perhaps say things they may later regret. Someone may also call a "time-out" if he or she feels that an *other person* is loosing or about to lose their temper. ***It is very important not to explain, at this time, why you are taking a time-out.*** Explaining *why* often leads to an argument about "Why I don't want to argue with you ..."Because you can be so pig-headed, stupid," or some other provocative statement. *[In professional sports, even with highly gifted and talented athletes," time-outs" are used to reassess what is happening, get back to one's original game plan, to discuss different strategies, as well as to just slow down the action.]*

Ed: Boy, can I relate to that!

Jim: Clarify that calling a "time-out" is not being disrespectful, providing that one does not overuse this tool and that the person who called the "time out" will attempt, within a reasonable period of time, to try to discuss the issue in a more constructive manner. A reasonable period can be flexible but generally could be within minutes, hours, or perhaps a few days later when the individual has been able to chill and think more clearly. ***It is also important to note that at the time someone calls a time-out the other person(s) does not have to be in agreement with the timing of the time- out. The other person(s) can continue to argue, if they so chose, without you present.***

"The Serenity Prayer" and slogans like, "One Day At a Time," "One Thing At a Time," and "Don't Go to Every Argument You Are Invited to," are technically called "mnemonic devices" or memory aids. There is a great deal of psychological and educational principles behind many of the slogans. These short phrases ***can help us to slow down our racing thoughts, manage our emotions better, and avoid a war zone mentality*** in which it seems that nearly everything turns into an argument. "First Things First," and "How Important Is It?" or some phrases that we make up ourselves, ***can help us to prioritize which issues we want to, or need to, deal with first, and which ones we can postpone for another time*** when we have the energy or objectivity to deal with them more constructively. Such mental tools can also help us to remember to also add praise and encouragement in more of our dealings with our children. It can also be helpful to catch ourselves when we feel the need to make a decision right away. Reacting to the teen's frequent sense of urgency…"But I need to know now" can often be a recipe for trouble.

Lynn: Recently at an Al-Anon meeting I heard someone say that it was helpful for him to remember "someone else's lack of planning is not my emergency." I am trying to remember that I don't always have to make an immediate decision, especially if I am angry or feeling frazzled.

Ed: I keep reacting to Kim when she has an attitude. **Just because she's unhappy about something, does not mean I have to take it**

personally. I'm trying to bite my tongue and ***let her be unhappy*** at times. I am also beginning to remind myself that "I Don't Have to Go to Every Argument I'm Invited to" and "Don't Try to Reason With an Unreasonable Person."

Lynn: *[Jokingly asks]* are you referring to me?

Ed: I think I ... I think I am going to try and change the subject. *[Laughs.]*

Jim: It can also be helpful when we remember that ***setting limits is about guiding and directing children and teens,*** helping them get better and better at catching themselves, and **helping *them, not* making *them, develop more effective emotional coping skills.*** What some refer to as ***"teachable moments" are periodic times when the teen, not the parent, is more ready and able to receive information that may be applicable to their situation.*** There are often other times when the teen is not with a parent(s) and is more able and ready to process information and experiences and develop additional insights.

It is not uncommon that many people initially come to an Al-Anon or Nar-Anon meeting to try to learn how to make the drinker or user stop and to look for others to tell them how to make that happen. Usually, other Al-Anon or Nar-Anon members will smile and share that they too thought that way when they first started to attend meetings. No one will tell another what to do, but instead will share what has helped him or her to better understand and cope with the drinker or user in their life. Some may also share examples of how they used to try to control someone else's drinking or using, or tried to find out if they started drinking or using again, and how it usually just made the situation worse, as well as increasing their own distress and heartache.

Some parents choose to write down certain agreements and limits in order to not rely on memory or the teen's "selective memory": "I never said I'd go to those stupid AA meetings; I said I'd think about it." It is important to note that this process includes what the parent(s) agree to do, such as participating in counseling and or attending Al-Anon. Try to remember to "Keep It Simple," start with a few issues and try to resist the urge to list everything that concerns you.

Another option is to have all parties sign a written agreement, thus turning it into a contract. This does not guarantee that the teenager will always abide by the agreement, but it does add to the level of commitment each person is willing to make. Increasing the teenager's and/or parents' level of commitment makes procrastinating, rationalizing or use of other defense mechanisms more difficult to use. ***If a teen refuses to sign a written agreement, don't argue with him or her. This may be an opportunity for everyone to chill for a while. Try to avoid the temptation of leaving a parting shot, such as "if you don't sign it, you can't go out next weekend either!"***

If you use written agreements or contracts, try to limit their use. Remember there isn't a perfect approach to parenting. Overuse of any approach can lead to becoming rigid and can result in more power struggles between parent and teen. Remember that recovery from alcohol and other drug dependencies (as with maturation) takes time and often involves a certain amount of testing of limits. Some things may need to be learned the hard way. We *could* see this as growing pains (for the teen and, perhaps, for the parent(s) too) and not failure. Recovery is a process, not an event, and, as stated in chapter 1, pain is often a great motivator for change. Isn't this why *you* started reading this book?

As we try to respect each other as individuals, it can also be helpful to recognize that each has certain rights.

Parents have a right to:

1. **Be human**, don't expect to be superhuman.
2. Be wrong, to make mistakes, and admit it—"I don't have to have all the answers, all of the time."
3. Your own physical and emotional well-being.
4. Stop blaming yourself for causing the disease.
5. Love your son or daughter ***and hate his or her disease or behavior.***
6. Get help for yourself.
7. Be an adult and manage your home as best you can.
8. Make rules and expect them to be followed.
9. Not go to every argument you are invited to.
10. Not accept unacceptable behavior.
11. Say no.
12. Say yes.

This is only a partial list. You also have a right to refuse help and expect others to "do as I say and not as I do." You also have a right to stay feeling angry, self-righteous, and depressed.

We also need to acknowledge and respect the **Teen's rights** as a person.

Your son or daughter has a right to:

1. Be sick, not bad.
2. Make mistakes.
3. Choose right from wrong.
4. Self-respect.
5. Feelings and opinions—whatever they may be.
6. Express their feelings and opinions, even if they seem naive.
7. Suffer the consequences of their actions.
8. Learn from their mistakes and/or ***learn at a slower pace than you would wish.***

Teens may need time to earn the car keys back or to re-earn your trust, but **they shouldn't need to earn your respect as a person.**

Teens do not have a right to:

1. Abuse themselves.
2. Abuse others.
3. Break the law, even though they have a disease.

Helping our teens learn more acceptable, healthier, and safer behaviors also involves ***communication.*** Effective communication involves assertive behaviors, standing up for oneself without putting others down, taking responsibility for our own feelings, while not criticizing someone else's feelings or trying to force someone to change. ***Basic communication styles include: assertive, non assertive, and aggressive.*** **Characteristics of assertive behavior include:**

1. Trying to state exactly what you think and feel, rather than beating around the bush and talking about everything else except the real issue(s).
2. Talk about one issue at a time. Remember "K.I.S.S.," "Keep It Simple, Sweetheart!"
3. "First Things First": state your point. Try to resist the urge to always explain or apologize. If an explanation is appropriate, you can give it ***after*** you have stated your opinion or feeling. Explanations are not always necessary. At the time you may not know why you feel the way you do. You do not always have to justify your opinions or feelings. This is an option you can choose to use or not use as long as you are trying the best you can.

Some examples of assertive comments are:

"Thank you for the compliment (instead of minimizing our deserving it)."
"***I*** don't agree with that opinion."
"***I*** would rather discuss this a little later. I am involved in something right now."
"That's not my responsibility. You'll have to deal with it."
"***I*** appreciate you concern, but I don't agree."
"***I*** don't like what you did (or said)."

Note that assertive statements often start with the word ***I***, rather than the word ***you***. ***I*** statements communicate more clearly and directly.

Reasons why some people are not assertive:

1. Not realizing we have a choice.
2. Seeing assertiveness as selfish or negative.
3. Blaming others.
4. Not knowing how to be assertive or what words to use.
5. It seems difficult.

Examples of counter-productive communication:

Passive: Avoidance—waiting for others to make our decisions. In the long run, this drains energy and usually causes more problems. For examples you say to yourself: "She should know how I feel" or "I'll let my husband or wife handle it."
Aggressive: Attacking another's opinion or self-esteem. Aggressive statements, tone of voice, or body language can often invite retaliation either immediately or later on. For example: Pointing a finger at another, "How can you act that way?" or "***You*** shouldn't feel that way." From a teen's perspective: "That's it. I'm out of here. ***You're*** a jerk." ***You*** statements often increase the likelihood of mutual defensiveness.

Short of tying your teen up and locking him or her in their room (it's OK to have thoughts like this, but we think it might be against the law in most communities), **we may need to accept that *some limits or guidelines cannot always be directly enforced.*** As one parent said to us, "we tried to enforce John's curfew, but he just leaves through his bedroom window." Instead she would attempt, either when the adolescent returned or perhaps the next day when things were calmer, to inform her son that his behavior was unacceptable and what the consequence was. At times, this could be an opportunity for a relatively calm discussion or perhaps an opportunity to state the consequence and then announce a time-out.

What we can do is:

1. Expect limits or rules to be followed.
2. Reinforce, in a positive way, the progress he or she has made.
3. Try to be consistent in allowing the teen to experience (within reason) the consequences of his or her actions.
4. Try to be realistic about how much our son or daughter can accomplish at one given time.
5. Try to be realistic about how much we are able to consistently follow up.

"**Easy Does It**." Try to go slow. If you feel as if you are going to lose it while talking to your son or daughter (or spouse or partner, the teen's teacher, or others), remember: "Say What You Mean, Mean What You Say, Without Saying It Mean." Ideally, if we cannot do all three, it may be more effective to wait a minute or two, or 2002, to regain our composure.

Ed: At a recent Al-Anon meeting that I went to the topic was Step 1: "We admitted we were powerless over alcohol—that our lives had become unmanageable."[4] *[In Nar-Anon: "We admitted we were powerless over drugs—that our lives had become unmanageable."]* I am beginning to accept that ***I am powerless over Kim's use of alcohol and drugs and that when I become obsessed with whether or not she is drinking or using, my life, my feelings, and my thinking become very unmanageable.*** I used to think that when Kim was drinking or using, my *wife* became unmanageable, but I am trying to focus on changing *myself* and not other people.

Lynn: Very funny. At times I need to go to a meeting without Ed and his sense of humor. I occasionally attend a Nar-Anon meeting. There is only one near us, but there seems to be more parents there. At one meeting I went to, someone read page 144 of *One Day At a Time in Al-Anon. [This is sometimes referred to as ODAT. Note that Nar-Anon uses the same books as Al-Anon, but the reader is encouraged to substitute the word "*drug*" wherever the word "*alcohol*" appears.* Nar-Anon *publishes many of its own pamphlets, which are available at Nar-Anon meetings]*: "Today's Reminder. I will apply the wisdom of the First Step not only to my relations to the alcoholic *[addict]*, but to all the people in my life. I will not attempt to manage or control what is clearly beyond my powers." Some days I need to remind myself, over and over, that I cannot control what Ed does or what comes out of his mouth.

Ed: Ouch. I resemble that remark.

Lynn: See what I have to put up with? [*Laughs]*.

Jim: I am not getting in the middle of this one. *[Laughs.]*

Chapter 5

WHY MY KID?

"Hugs, not drugs," was a popular bumper sticker at one time. My friend Kathy, a mother of a recovering alcohol -dependent son, ***and*** daughter, once told me she used to cry when she saw those words. "Do people think my kids were drinking and drugging because I didn't hug them or love them enough?" Kathy and her husband are both recovering alcoholics and became involved in AA when their children were very young. Their son told me he had no memories of when his parents were still drinking or using. Growing up as a young child, he knew he had loving parents who were very committed to staying sober. He and his sister actually had been to many AA meetings with their parents, never picturing themselves abusing alcohol or other drugs let alone becoming dependent as well!

What did I do wrong? What could I have done differently? It often seems we parents automatically blame ourselves when something happens to one of our children. Harold Kushner in *When Bad Things Happen to Good People* notes that "why" isn't always a question. Sometimes it is a cry of pain. Some parents' report they have felt that some relatives, neighbors, and even some professionals have blamed them for their teen's drinking and/or using. It may seem like rubbing salt into a wound. Other times parents, well-intended friends, family, and some professionals appear to dwell on why the alcohol- or other drug-dependent person is drinking or using.

"There must be some deep psychological reason that he or she is self-medicating. A number of studies suggest that many alcohol- and/or other drug-dependent individuals have a significantly higher incidence of additional or "co-occurring" mental health issues such as depression, anxiety disorders, including post traumatic stress disorders, as well as attention deficit hyperactivity disorder and other learning difficulties. While it may not always be initially clear which problem came first, many treatment programs and therapists now recognize that recovery rates appear to increase when substance abuse or dependence and certain mental health issues are addressed concurrently, that is, at the same time. Good treatment begins with good assessment. *[See "How to Find Experienced Help", free, at suspendedadolescence.com.]*

There have been a number of studies trying to determine if there is a pre-alcoholic, or *pre-drug-dependent personality,* that could hopefully be identified with interventions developed ***before*** a person develops problems with alcohol or drug abuse or dependence. At this time, ***no one has been able to predict who will become an alcoholic or drug addict.*** While it is of the utmost importance for researchers to continue to understand factors contributing to substance abuse and dependence, focusing primarily on the "whys" of the problem during treatment may feed into the drinker or user's defenses and take the focus off of the main problem. Whether the alcoholic or other drug-dependent person has other problems or not, ***things will most likely not***

get better as long as they continue to drink and/or use. Many of their problems are the* result *of their drinking and using and not the* cause *of the drinking or using. Problems not caused by the drinking or using are usually made worse by it.

It has been known by many professionals going back a number of decades that alcohol and other drug dependencies appear to be more common in certain families. Recent research reports that 50 to 60 percent of the risk for alcoholism may be genetically determined for both men and women. "Genes alone do not preordain that someone will be an alcoholic; features in the environment along with gene-environment interactions account for the remainder of the risk."[11]

In my family (Jerry), my maternal grandfather's alcoholism emerged during the period of Prohibition. He made wine in the basement. Fortunately, he was treated by a physician during the early 1940s who told him and my parents that alcoholism was a disease and that ***it was the first drink that would lead back to compulsive drinking***. It would be decades later that researchers would better understand the chemistry of addiction. My grandfather lived many sober years afterward, for which I am very grateful. I sometimes wish there was a law that if alcoholism and/or another drug dependency happens in a family, then we should be automatically exempt from having to deal with it again. Unfortunately, illnesses that have a hereditary component can have a greater chance of occurring in other relatives. Alcoholism doesn't run in my in my family—it gallops.

Genetic susceptibility is also involved in many other diseases. It has been long known that certain other illnesses like diabetes occur more often in certain families. ***It is also important to note that although certain diseases may have a tendency to be more common in certain families, in the case of addictions, the majority of children and grandchildren of an alcoholic*** **do not develop ongoing problems with alcohol or drugs themselves!** Alcoholism, drug dependencies, diabetes, and certain other diseases can and do also occur when there is no family history of these diseases. *[See chapter 7, "Letting Go."]* It is, however, imperative that family members make an effort to become aware of symptoms they themselves may have with the respective disease. It is not uncommon that when one member of a family is initially diagnosed with an illness that may have a hereditary component, another family member may have symptoms of an earlier or less disruptive stage of the same illness. Generally speaking, ***the earlier an illness or condition is identified and treated the better.*** Family members of an alcoholic or other drug-dependent person may need to examine their own use of alcohol or other prescribed or non-prescribed drugs.

In order to clarify your relationship to your use of alcohol or other drugs, we suggest you take a few moments to answer the following questions.

SECTION A

1. Have you ever spent more money than you could afford on alcohol or other drugs? **Yes No**
2. Have you ever lost time from work as a result of drinking or using or gone into work hung over? **Yes No**
3. Have other people criticized your drinking or using? **Yes No**
4. Have drinking or using ever negatively affected your reputation? **Yes No**
5. Has a spouse or romantic partner ever threatened to leave if you didn't stop or cut down? **Yes No**
6. Have you ever been injured while you have been drinking or using? **Yes No**
7. Have you ever been arrested for driving under the influence of alcohol or other drugs? **Yes No**
8. Have you ever felt guilty after drinking or using? **Yes No**
9. Have you ever gotten angry at yourself the morning after you drank or used? **Yes No**
10. Have you ever had periods when you were drinking or using (without passing out) when you couldn't remember all or a significant part of what you had done or how you got home? **Yes No**

RESPONSES: Section A

Total Yes: ____________________ **Total No:** ____________________

SECTION B

1. Have you ever tried to completely abstain from drinking or using other drugs? **Yes No**
2. Have you ever tried to cut down on your alcohol or other drug use? **Yes No**
3. Have you attempted to control your alcohol or drug use by trying to set limits on how much you use in one evening or one day? **Yes No**
4. Have you tried switching from one drug to another (for example, stop drinking and use tranquilizers or marijuana to relax) or switching from mixed drinks or vodka to wine or beer? **Yes No**
5. Have you lost interest in leisure activities that do not involve alcohol or other drugs? **Yes No**
6. When you are not drinking or using other drugs, do you find yourself thinking about when you can drink or use again? **Yes No**
7. Do you usually prefer the company of people who like to drink or use the way you like to instead of being with abstainers or people who "nurse" their drinks? **Yes No**
8. Do you get high on alcohol and/or other drugs when you are alone? **Yes No**
9. Are you able to consume a larger amount of alcohol or other drugs before you start feeling it? **Yes No**
10. Are smaller amounts of alcohol or other drugs starting to cause you as much or even more trouble than the larger amounts used to? **Yes No**
11. Do you periodically drink or use drugs before lunch? **Yes No**

RESPONSES: Section B

Total Yes: ________________ **Total No:** ____________________

Section A Evaluation

Fill in the totals from Section A

Total **Yes** responses: ________

Total **No** responses: ________

Yes answers in Section A are indicators of a significant drinking or drug problem. If your alcohol or other drug use repeatedly interferes in one or more areas in your life, ***You have a drinking and/or drug-abuse problem.***

Section B Evaluation

Fill in the totals from Section B

Total **Yes** responses: ________

Total **No** responses: ________

Yes answers in Section B are indicators of an emotional and/or physical dependency on alcohol and or/other drugs. Questions 1 to 4 deal with attempts to control alcohol or other drug use. No one tries to control something ***unless it is in need of control.*** Questions 5 to 8 indicate a growing preoccupation or obsession with alcohol and/or other drugs. As alcoholism or other drug dependencies progress, life revolves more and more around drinking or using or thinking about drinking or using. Questions 9 to 11 are symptoms of advanced third-stage alcoholism or drug dependence.

Some parents comment to us: "I use marijuana myself. I don't think I abuse it. I just have a joint after work, like someone else might have one or two drinks." It is important to recognize the difference between how beverages containing alcohol and other drugs are used.

Drugs, including prescription medications, are taken by *dosage*. A *dose* is a specified amount to achieve a desired effect. In the case of taking an antibiotic, the desired effect would be to fight an infection. Marijuana, cocaine, and other mood-altering drugs are also taken in an amount to achieve a desired effect ... to get high. In having one or two drinks with a meal or snacks, the desired effect may be to enjoy the beverage and not necessarily drinking it to get a high. Using alcohol or other drugs to get high or feeling really good impairs judgment and increases the risk of becoming emotionally and/or physically dependent on the substance.

When parents get high on marijuana or alcohol, it is sending a message to kids that it is alright to take something to change the way you feel and alter your perception of reality, just as long as you don't get into trouble. When someone drinks to feel good or uses other drugs to get high, they are thinking about getting high and either don't think about potential problems or will often rationalize the action with thoughts like "I'll be careful," "I know how to handle myself," or "I'm just having a good time, it's not like I need this stuff."

You don't want to hurt your children. Few parents do. But double standards don't fly anymore: they never really did. ***If it is hard for you to deal honestly with your drinking or drug use, just think how hard it is for your teenager.***

If you think you may have a problem with drinking or other drug use, remember ***you are not a bad parent, you are a human being who needs some help! [See suspendedadolescence.com article "Finding Experienced Help" available at no charge.] You can also check your local phone book, call directory assistance for alcoholics anonymous or narcotics anonymous, or try to find help on-line***: ***AA, alcoholics-anonymous.org, or NA,na.org.***

PART III

PROGRESS

Chapter 6

PROGRESS NOT PERFECTION

Margo, a parent, states: "It has been a while now since Michael went for help and our family is in remission, slowly gaining strength and recovering from what the disease has done to all of us. I still feel that sense of panic and fear every time Michael is not home on time or when he has forgotten to leave a note telling me where he is. It took us four long years to reach bottom, so I guess I can't expect recovery overnight."

Many alcohol, or other drug-dependent people, who are exposed to appropriate treatment, *do* achieve ***remission. Remission*** of this illness is living clean and sober (abstinent from alcohol and "*all*" other drugs), "One Day At a Time." Certainly no one really wants to think about relapse. As with any other illness, relapse can occur. To deny that relapse is a possibility is to allow denial of this illness to get in the way of the recovery process.

Recovery from illnesses often progresses differently for each person. Some people need more help, time, and experience than others to achieve their goal. This is particularly true for teenagers. They usually don't have the same life experiences and coping skills as older people. ***As was mentioned earlier in chapter 4, certain areas of a teenager's brain are still physically maturing until they are in their early twenties.*** Because of these factors, teens often need more time to acquire the skills and understanding necessary to care for their illness. Teenagers are also more inclined than adults to test the chronicity or limits of their illness. This does *not* mean they have totally rejected treatment. Much of that stays with them even when they may not want to admit it. **Exposure to treatment, including AA and NA, initiates some change even though at times we may not be able to see it. The recovery process has begun.**

Lynn: Treatment didn't work. Kim started drinking again. What did I do wrong?

Jim: You didn't do anything wrong. Kim has an illness, one that can result in a relapse if she does not accept that she is powerless over mood-altering substances and that she needs help. You couldn't make her stop drinking or using. What makes you think you could prevent her from choosing to drink or use again?

Lynn: Every now and then I catch myself blaming myself and also trying to control her illness. Will I ever stop doing that? I should know better by now!

Jim: Lynn, you are human! Where is it written that parents never make mistakes, get discouraged, or feel scared?

Lynn: I know, but sometimes I just need to hear it again ... that it's not my fault, that I'm doing the right things.

Jim: I'd suggest that you occasionally attend open AA and/or NA meetings. *[See suspendedadolescence.com articles "What to expect at an Al-Anon or Nar-Anon meeting" and "What to expect at an AA or NA meeting," both offered at no charge.]* What you'll probably hear is something like "When I made up my mind to take that first drink or drug, *nothing* could have stopped me." ***What you will hear and see are many, many people of all ages who are staying clean and sober and not picking up that first drink or other drug.*** In early recovery, alcohol, and other drug-dependent people struggle with understanding and accepting that, regardless of their age or which drug they pick up (including alcohol even if one is of legal drinking age), it is the first one that starts a ***chemical compulsion in their brain*** that will sooner, rather than later, lead to taking another and another drink or joint or line. This is the single most significant way in which alcoholics and drug-dependent people differ from everyone else. ***Alcoholism and other drug dependencies are very democratic!*** Although the rates of these illnesses may vary somewhat from culture to culture, these illnesses wreak havoc in all societies, throughout the world. Some people, especially teenagers, often need more time than others to accept that they are powerless over alcohol and other drugs and that they need help.

Ed: I can relate to that. I had stopped going to my meetings, and, when Kim relapsed, I blamed myself. Then I was mad at you, Al-Anon, and AA because I tried to follow all of the suggestions and she still got high. I even found myself thinking: "It's those damn kids she is hanging around with again. Where the hell are their parents while they are out drinking and using?" Probable worn out and worried sick like I was. I thought I had accepted that I couldn't control her illness, but I guess I have to keep working on it. I guess we family members have slips to.

Jim: Can you see your own progress?

Ed: Yeah. If this had happened before I started going to meetings, I wouldn't have slept for days. I would have also taken my frustrations out on Kim and the rest of the family.

Jim: But you didn't take it out on the others—just on yourself.

Ed: *[Laughs.]* You know I find myself laughing more often too, even though it's still hard at times. I've been getting more out of my meetings lately. Maybe I'm clearing up too.

Jim: *[Laughs.]* Hang in there Dad. You *are* doing alright.

Lynn: Worrying about the future must be working because most of the things I worry about that might happen, don't. *[Laughs.]* Kim mentioned recently that she noticed I "wasn't such a bitch lately." That's the closest I've come to an outright compliment from her in a long time! You know, the day after she got high, she was so quiet. I think she really felt remorse.

Jim: She's a sick kid, not a bad kid.

When someone is recovering from a serious illness or injury, we may notice that certain aspects of a person's functioning are improving. However, because they are not "fully recovered," it also means that there are still signs and symptoms of the actual illness. One of the great difficulties is not knowing if someone will continue to improve, a step at a time, or maybe even an "inch at a time," or will return to their regular pattern of drinking or using or use even more.

A friend of ours is a recovering alcoholic and a retired clergyman. He had been in and out of AA for quite some time and had even been in a number of detoxification and residential treatment programs. He told us that the last time he had been in a treatment program his recovery started even though he didn't stay sober. He explained that something finally sunk in. He knew he couldn't keep drinking as much as he had been. He began to attend AA a number of times a week, but he would periodically drink before he went to a meeting and sometimes after he returned from a meeting. He said "I can understand today that some people might have thought I was being hypocritical by going to meetings even if I had been drinking or drinking on my way home from a meeting. But I really wanted what the other AA members had … peace of mind … and serenity. It took me another year of going to meetings before I realized that in order for things to change in my life, ***I needed to not take the first drink.***" This may sound kind of strange. How could it take so long for him to figure that out? He also described how toward the end of his active alcoholic drinking, he would often use a breath-spray ***before he returned phone calls*** to his parishioners so they wouldn't know he had been drinking. "At the time it made sense to me," he said.

By attending a number of open AA and/or NA meetings, with or without your teen, family members can gain insight into how powerful and insidious addictions can be as well as how clouded or impaired alcoholics' and addicts' thinking can become.

Many of us have been raised as children to try to understand others by putting yourself in their shoes. Although that is often good advice, sometimes it backfires. When a non-alcoholic or non- drug-dependent person tries to think about how the alcoholic or addict might feel or why he or she acts the way they do, we are usually going to come up with a non-alcoholic or a non-drug-dependent efforts at using logical thinking. ***Alcoholics and other drug-dependent people, whether they are still actively drinking or using or are in very early recovery, don't often think logically. It takes time to recover*** from the effects of repeated abuse of alcohol and other drugs. It can take several months or longer for the brain to clear up or heal.

It also takes time for parents to acquire the skills and understanding necessary to effectively cope with someone else's alcohol and drug dependence. Parents **can help** ***their sons and daughters learn*** **from their experiences even though** ***they*** **can't make** ***them learn.*** Encouraging your child, not enabling, setting examples, and many other actions can have a very significant effect on a teenager. You are doing alright folks. Keep on trying and learning.

Lenny, another friend of ours, who was a self-admitted recovering alcoholic, contributed the following:

These two Chinese characters mean ***“trouble”*** *and* ***“crisis.”***

機

Trouble

會

Crisis

When combined, these two characters mean OPPORTUNITY. If you use Al-Anon, Nar-Anon, and/or other help one step at a time, ***you, too, can create OPPORTUNITIES.***

CHAPTER 7

LETTING GO

Someone once said: "No Pain, No Gain." On locker room walls this edict loudly proclaims that the way to succeed is to work hard and experience some pain. Could this mean that sometimes pain is good, helpful and even necessary?

Certainly nobody wants pain in their lives. However, when it does occur, you can turn that feeling from a negative, depressing experience into a positive, spirit-strengthening power in your life. It begins with the acceptance of pain, at times, as part of being human. Scott Peck, a Harvard-trained psychiatrist, begins his book, *The Road Less Traveled*, with this sentence: "*Life is difficult.*" He goes on to say that this is a great paradox because once we accept it, we transcend it. Comparing our lot in life to others who seem more fortunate serves as an enormous hurdle in coping with the situation in a more effective way. Once we accept the fact that life is difficult, it begins to lose its power over us. The fact that it is_difficult no longer matters.

Peck is sharing two thoughts with us. The first is that many of us spend much of our lives running from problems and pain. While this is a natural reaction, in the long run it often causes more suffering than it avoids. Secondly, in spending our energy and time denying or avoiding pain, we prevent ourselves from reaching resources we have within us for overcoming the problems we face. God or some higher power has given us enormous reserves of creativity, which we may never tap if we spend our time refusing to accept the portion of pain that is part of life. If we use tactics of avoidance, if we numb ourselves with alcohol or other drugs, or if we simply refuse to acknowledge the pain, we only make matters worse, by adding deception to the mix.

Harold Kushner writes in his book, *When Bad Things Happen to Good People*, that "Pain is the price we pay for being alive. Dead cells—our hair, fingernails—can't feel pain; they cannot feel anything. When we understand that, our question will change from 'Why do we feel pain?' to 'What do we do with our pain' so that it becomes meaningful and not just pointless, empty suffering."

One resource we have when we are felling bad is the inner ability to separate the *essential* from the *nonessential.* Remembering to "*Keep It Simple*," "*First Things First*," or *"How Important Is It,"* can help us to place problems in their true perspective. Pain can put us in touch with deep, inner resources. Some of the most powerful masterpieces of mankind have been created by composers, artists, and architects who have experienced tremendous anguish.

Painful feelings and events often tend to confuse us, but they can also clarify and purify our thoughts. Alcohol and other drugs, however, can confuse and short circuit creativity by temporarily disguising feelings. A number of literary greats serve as examples of this short-circuiting process. Ernest Hemingway, William Faulkner, F. Scott Fitzgerald,

Jack London, and Dylan Thomas are all examples of how some form of alcohol or drug abuse eventually interfered with their ability to constructively use emotional turmoil in creative ways. For teenagers, the ***pain*** they experience during the progression of their illness and recovery process, ***is preparing them for a richer life***. It is extremely important and helpful to remember this.

An additional resource that our trials can force up from the depths of our being ***is creativity.*** Someone who has never known real deprivation has never been driven to the limits. Consequently, he or she has not had to dig for new and creative ways to survive. Haven't you been impressed when watching the Olympics how we often hear of competitors who started out with some handicap? Isn't it amazing when a young woman born without arms becomes a fine artist? Doesn't it boggle your mind to learn of a musician who is blind?

These are not coincidences. Adversity has challenged them to probe the depths of their reserves. Most of us don't know how much we can accomplish because we've not had to dig deeply enough. This does not mean we haven't tried hard enough; it may mean we have been spending vast amounts of time and energy and not getting the results we want. We may see feelings of hurt as a curse, but with help they can become a blessing in disguise. These feeling often prove to us the almost limitless possibilities we have. Hope and faith can be the liberating forces—even in the midst of pain—that open new possibilities. Most defeat has within it the seeds of recovery!

Pain can not only put you in touch with your untapped reserves, it may also lead you and the teen to real maturity. Feeling your pain is an inevitable part of being human. ***Suffering is optional!*** Parents who try to smooth out every bump in the road for their children enable them to exist in a state of ***suspended adolescence,* or dependence.** It's not easy to see our children in pain, but the longer you delay that inevitable lesson about life, the greater disservice you do them and yourself.

Letting go is a very uncomfortable thing for all of us to do, especially parents. It goes against parental instinct. For many years we nurtured, cared for, worried and even agonized over this child who now seems to care little or nothing about others. Here is where learning how to let go of the unessentials becomes so important.

There comes a time as a parent when we simply must let go of certain issues. As parents of minors, we are responsible for their physical and emotional well-being, but the responsibility for the consequences of the teen's actions belong to him or her. Smothering your adolescent can deter and/or divert their learning process and burn you out at the same time. By letting go, you are more able to redirect your love in more helpful ways, which can prove to be more supportive and productive in the long run.

Dr. DeSantis, one of the authors of this book, shares the following personal experience:

A number of years ago, I developed an interest in sailing. After several frightening and embarrassing attempts at learning this skill through reading a how-to book, I decided a few lessons from an experienced sailor were in order. To this day, I am grateful for those few hours spent with someone knowledgeable. This became especially clear as the winds got stronger or when I felt I was beginning to lose control of my direction on the boat. The feelings of frustration and fear were overpowering when I sensed that the wind was taking me farther and farther from the shore. Obviously, I needed help. Each time the wind grew stronger, I grew more tense. As I held on tightly to the rope attached to the sail, the boat would tip onto its side, farther and farther, until it seemed the water would breach the side of the boat and come pouring in. It also seemed the wind could simply push the boat over, and I would lose complete control of the boat as I sank to the bottom. A whole range of sensations filled me even though I knew how to swim and was wearing a life preserver at the time.

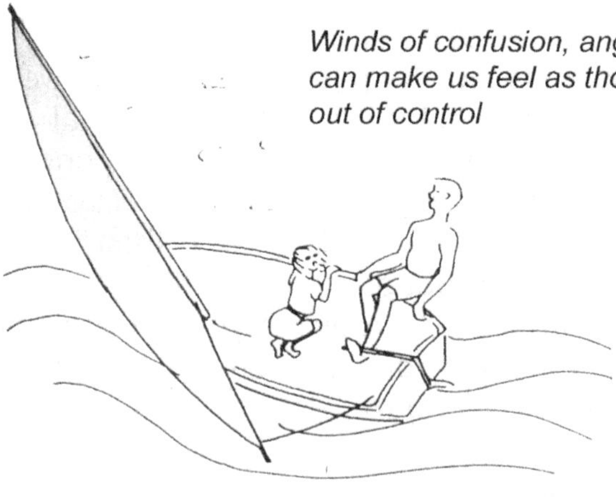

Winds of confusion, anger and pain can make us feel as though we are out of control

My instructor informed me early on that the most effective way to react to the strong winds or the uncomfortable feeling of tipping over was to simply ***let go of the rope.*** Letting go of the rope seemed to go against every instinct I had. How could I control the boat, and my fate, if I let go of the rope? The rope was the only control I had left, or so I thought. Following a few timid attempts, I learned why letting go works.

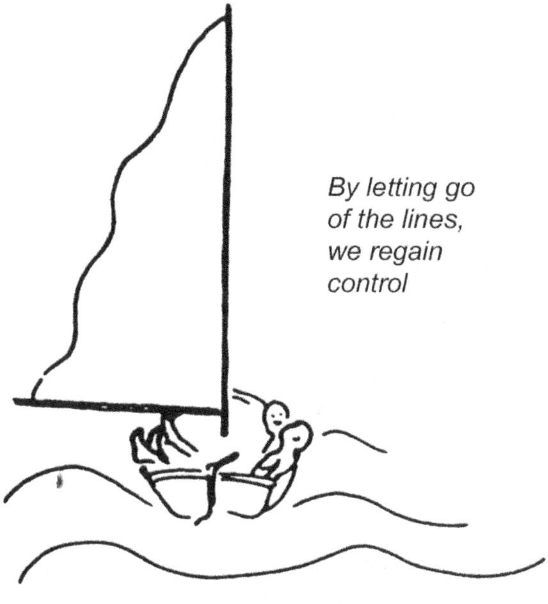

As I let go, much to my joy, the boat came upright and was no longer tipping far to one side. It still bobbed around and rose and fell with each wave, but I did not sense that it would tip over. The boat automatically began to face the wind and even seemed to ride the waves joyfully, going up and over each one.

The next thing that happened completely surprised me. As I sat in the boat and it headed into the wind, I realized the sail and the boom (poles that the sail is attached to) were also coming into line with the boat, so that now the rope, which I had let go of moments ago and was just out of reach, was now dangling above me, easily within reach.

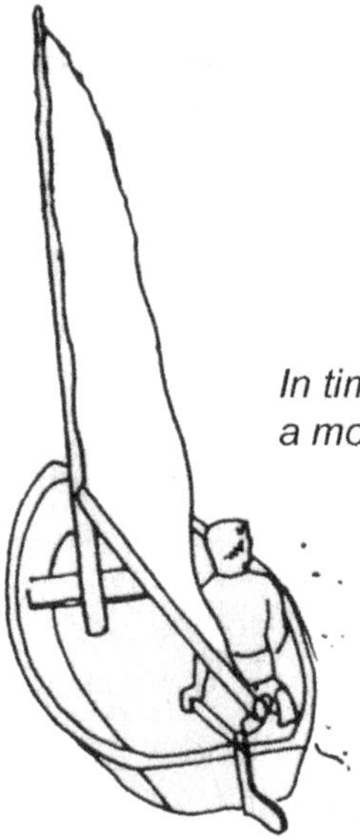

In time, we are able to set a more effective course

As we consider the analogy of the sailboat and the exercise of letting go, we may feel that the confusion of living with alcoholism or drug dependence is beginning to overcome us as we attempt to control the situation. By letting go, we actually regain control of ourselves so that we are able to be more effective and helpful.

It is important to let go of the past. Past errors, mistakes of judgment, and events all tend to keep wounds open and set up barriers against feeling better. Dwelling on the past will only serve to continue the cycle. Today, this moment is all that can be lived.

Try this experiment. Light a candle, let it burn for a few moments, then blow it out. A column of smoke will rise from the wick for awhile. If you light a match and hold it in the column of smoke an inch or so above the wick, the flame will travel down the smoke and reignite the candle. That same principle can apply to the past. When we dwell on disturbing events, it becomes more difficult to live in the present. ***Letting go* doesn't mean putting all the responsibility on the alcoholic or drug-dependent person, and washing our hands of the situation. *It doesn't mean stop caring*.**

We need to find a balance between (1) avoidance of share responsibility for recovery and (2) feeling responsibility for all the ills and imperfections of our children. A client of ours once said "By the time I let go of something, it has scratches and claw marks all over it."

A parent, in response to reading *Suspended Adolescence* writes:

> Our daughter's drug dependence was uncovered when she was 16. We tried all kinds of professional intervention and succeeded only when we began to use the principles of the Al-Anon program. Counselors not familiar with alcoholism were not very helpful. We took drastic kinds of action, which I would never have believed myself capable of, and it worked. I thought you might appreciate feedback from our daughter directly so I asked her "What did we do, as parents, that most helped you realize your need for help when you were drinking and drugging?" Her answers: "When you detached yourself from me, and I had to stop blaming you and face myself, was the most important in the

> beginning. When I got straight, what was most beneficial was that I knew you were supporting me—not making me feel worse than I already felt. You weren't angry with me. You gave me some distance and space to move and make my own choices.

An Al-Anon leaflet about detachment states:

> Detachment is neither kind nor unkind. It does not imply judgment or condemnation of the person or situation from which we are detaching. It is simply a means that allows us to separate ourselves from the adverse effects that another person's alcoholism can have upon our lives. Detachment helps families look at their situations realistically and objectively, thereby making intelligent decisions possible.

We have discussed a number of issues and made many suggestions throughout this book. In the final analysis, that which often blocks our ability to cope with a difficult situation or make any progress, is our own inability to let go of self-destructive thoughts that don't help anyone, least of all ourselves.

Bringing a book such as this to an end was difficult until we realized that this isn't the end. It is a beginning—a beginning that may help us see others differently and understand ourselves more deeply.

THE END—AND A NEW BEGINNING

BIBLIOGRAPHY

1. United States, Confidentiality Federal Regulations, CFR 42, http://www.treatment.org/taps/tap13.
2. The 2005 National Survey on Drug Use and Health (United States) estimated that 9.1 percent of people age 12 and older were classified with substance dependence or abuse disorders based upon criteria specified in the Diagnostic and Statistical Manual of Mental Disorders, 4th edition (DSM-IV). http://www.oas.samhsa.gov/nsduh.htm
3. http://www.pathwayscourses.samhsa.gov
4. http://www.al-anon.alateen.org/
5. http://www.nar-anon.org
6. http://www.familiesanonymous.org
7. Kushner, Harold S., When Bad Things Happen to Good People, Avon Book, New York, NY, 1981.
8. http://www.alcoholics-anonymous.org
9. http://www.mentalhelp.net/self-help
10. http://www.na.org
11. Alcohol Alert, NIAAA No. 60, July 2003, NIAAA Director Ting-Kai, MD.

APPENDIX

LETTING GO

To “let go” does not mean to stop caring, it means I can’t do it for someone else.

To ‘let go” is not to cut myself off, it’s the realization I can’t control another.

To “let go” is not to enable, but to allow learning from natural consequences.

To “let go” is to admit powerlessness, which means the outcome is not in my hands.

To “let go” is not to try to change or blame another, it’s to make the most of myself.

To “let go” is not to care for, but to care about.

To ‘let go” is not to fix, but to be supportive.

To “let go” is not to judge, but to allow another to be a human being.

To “let go” is not to be in the middle arranging all the outcomes, but to allow others to affect their own destinies.

To “let go” is not to be protective, it’s to permit another to face reality.

To “let go” is not to deny, but to accept.

To “let go” is not to nag, scold, or argue, but instead to search out my own shortcomings and correct them.

To “let go” is not to adjust everything to my desires, but to take each day as it comes, and cherish myself in it.

To “let go” is not to regret the past, but to grow and live for the future.

To “let go” is to fear less and love more.

Author Unknown

Made in the USA
Monee, IL
04 November 2026

67380498R00056